CHURCHES

> **Acts 2:42-47:**
>
> "They devoted themselves to
> the apostles' teaching and to fellowship, to the
> breaking of bread and to prayer. Everyone was
> filled with awe at the many wonders and signs
> performed by the apostles. All the believers were
> together and had everything in common. They
> sold property and possessions to give to anyone
> who had need. Every day they continued to meet
> together in the temple courts. They broke bread
> in their homes and ate together with glad and
> sincere hearts, praising God and enjoying the
> favor of all the people. And the Lord added to
> their number daily those who were being saved".

I love this passage. It is one of the earliest and purest descriptions of the church found in the New Testament. Believers meeting and living life together, but not just in buildings. Not just on Sundays. Not just in a church service. They met continually as they tried to learn how to live out the way of Jesus in every aspect of their lives. They had everything in common; not because they all looked the same, had the same personality type, the same gifts, or the same passions, but because Jesus was at the center of everything they did. This does not mean that everyone fit into a cookie cutter mold. In fact, we know it was messy and confusing at times.

MICRO CHURCH LEADER *Essentials*

A MICROCHURCH LEADER FIELD GUIDE

MATT ULRICH

INTRODUCTION

Jesus knew His mission had to continue long after His three and a half year ministry career would end. He knew he would need to invest Himself into others so that His message would endure from generation to generation until His return.

Although they did not really get it while He was with them, the disciples were able to piece together what Jesus taught them through the leading of the Holy Spirit and successfully raise up apprentices and disciple makers just as Jesus had done with them.

They carried with them the sense of urgency to invest into the next generation who has invested into the next generation who has invested into the next generation. And thanks to the commitment throughout the ages of disciples investing into apprentices, the mission of Jesus carries on to this day.

Now we are called to play our part in the mission of God and continue the legacy of making disciples. And if we want that to continue after we are gone, then we have to be relentless in our pursuit of pouring into others and making disciples who are going to make disciples.

We are not just looking for people with great strategies and microchurch structures; we are looking for those who are so smitten with Jesus they would give everything to see others taste and see that He is good. We want disciple makers who can't get their eyes off Jesus and desire others to know God and be known by God the way they have.

We want followers of Jesus so consumed by His love that it simply overflows into everything they do and say. We want disciples with lives so compelling that others are drawn into the kingdom of God because of what they see.

This cannot be done in our own strength; we must be radically committed to the daily apprenticeship and life-long training with Jesus, the ultimate disciple maker and lover of our souls. We must be open and willing to allow the Holy Spirit to teach, train, and lead us and allow ourselves to be transformed into the image of our Creator.

We want radical, real-deal disciple makers who are going to go and make more disciple makers, thereby fulfilling the Great Commission Jesus gave to His church.

WE ARE PRAYING *FOR YOU* IN THIS LIFE LONG PURSUIT!

Maybe even most of the time. Leaders made mistakes. There were sharp disagreements (Galatians 2:11-12). But they were in it for the right reasons - loving God and loving people - and this commonality of passion for Him is what united them.

But even in this raw, organic pursuit of Jesus the early church developed a bare bones structure that has been successfully used throughout church history. Their way of discipleship could be transferred and caught regardless of the socio-political landscape, making it immune to any backlash or persecution:

They met together in the temple courts and broke bread in their homes...

What a beautiful representation of how the early disciples lived out the way of Jesus: worshipping together, on mission together, and in community with one another. In the temple but also in their homes. In both their public life and in their private lives. There was a macro expression of the church gathering as well as micro expressions. There was an extended family of the faith that transcended any boundaries or barriers that would have traditionally held them back and kept Jews and Gentiles from coming together. It was counter-cultural. It was untraditional. It was beautiful.

We at the Greenhouse are so moved by this depiction of the early church that we are devoted to seeing this 1st century reality manifested in the

21st century church.

We recognize that it is not only the structure that brings life but a focus, love and desperation for Jesus. We understand that you can build it and they might not come, which is why we are not putting our trust in buildings, programs, or the newest church conference hype.

We are simply trying to reconnect with the ways the early church practiced radical, life-on-life discipleship that ended up changing our world forever.

Enter the microchurch.

It's not that we are opposed to Sunday morning gatherings. If lost people are hearing about Jesus, followers of Jesus are being refreshed, and souls are being recalibrated with His rhythms, we celebrate. We don't think that traditional weekend gatherings are a bad thing; we just don't think they are the only thing.

Faith is more than just Sundays. Discipleship is not simply taught; it is caught. Jesus told His disciples to follow Him, and for the next three years they did. Paul told his disciples to follow him as he followed Christ. And he didn't just mean when church gatherings were taking place. In the same way, we are calling disciples to a 24/7 lifestyle... because Sundays alone won't cut it.

This is why we take the Acts 2 both/and approach to church life. We believe there are things the macrochurch (weekend gatherings) can do that the microchurch cannot. We also believe there are things that can happen at the microchurch gathering which are crucial for real discipleship to take place; things that simply cannot happen at the macrochurch gathering. We believe both of these types of expressions have a place in creating an authentic discipleship culture that captures the essence of the Acts 2 church.

Microchurches are where the saints get equipped to do the work of the ministry. We have to be honest: not everyone is called to lead to 100, 1,000 or 10,000 people. But there are many followers of Jesus who are called to lead smaller expressions of 5, 10, or 30. (Our brothers and sisters in the Chinese and South Korean churches have tapped into this truth, as they have seen hundreds of thousands of micro church expressions multiply and flourish in the past century.) There are many gifts that do not have a place at a weekend gathering, but are vital and essential for the church to be fully expressed in a microchurch setting.

We want radical hospitality, spiritual gifts stirred regularly, and discipleship that is lived out in the context of real life and real community.

The way of Jesus is the way of discipleship, and discipleship doesn't happen without regular interactions with the church (i.e. the people - you are the church) throughout the week.

Microchurches are where this type of life-on-life discipleship becomes a reality, and to accomplish this kind of community we have put all our eggs in the microchurch basket; we want them to be excellent. We want them to be the best place to learn about Jesus and grow in your walk with Him. We also want microchurch leaders who are confident and equipped to launch, lead, grow, and multiply microchurches. If this is the way we make disciples, then let's make sure we set up our microchurches to have maximum discipleship impact while keeping our hearts and eyes focused on Jesus, which is why we wrote this book: to help you lead in a way that is going to produce radical disciples who are going to make radical disciples.

SO LET'S BEGIN...

Reflection Questions: Why Microchurches?

If someone asked you why we have microchurches at our church, what would you say?

What do microchurches bring to the table that the weekend gatherings do not?

How would you describe our commitment to both the weekend gathering and micro church gatherings to someone who wasn't "in the know"?

What is it about microchurches that makes it resistant to backlash or persecution?

2 LIVING IN THE GREEN

Living in the Green.

Get used to hearing that, because that is our discipleship M.O. around here. We live and breathe green discipleship. If you prick us, we bleed green. Why? Because we want disciples. Radical, sold-out, Holy Spirit-filled, justice-loving, lost-chasing, God-seeking disciples. And when someone actually catches this vision, his or her life turns green.

Why green?
Because:

yellow
+
blue
────
green

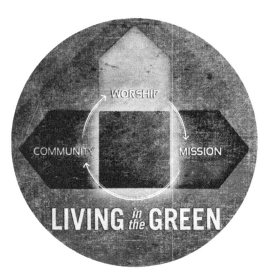

Let me explain:

We break down our relationships as vertical and horizontal relationships.

Our primary relationship is the one we have with God. This is represented by a vertical yellow arrow. We call this **WORSHIP**: not just the songs we sing on the weekend at our large group gatherings, but the lifestyle we live. You see, when you really worship something, it gets your everything... your time, your affection, your money, your talents, your devotion.... everything.

It doesn't matter what you say you worship; it matters what your life says you worship.

And when you love God with all your heart, soul, mind, and strength, true worship happens; it pours into everything you do. Everything becomes Jesus-centered and Gospel-driven. Your first love, your primary focus, is nothing other than Jesus, Jesus, Jesus. You live differently when you are walking in step with the Spirit. You find out who you are and what you are created for in Christ. You start living out of the overflow and your inner man/woman, that new creation inside of you, takes control. Jesus is on the throne and calling the shots. You are no longer in control. You willingly, joyfully, honorably give Jesus the rightful place on the throne of your heart and life.

You truly begin to worship. And when you truly begin to worship, you can't help it; it starts to affect the horizontal relationships you have with the people around you. It stirs your heart to do something that is beyond yourself. You start to tap into and yearn to fulfill the call of God on your life and to start partaking in the story that is greater than any other story, the redemptive story of God. And God sets your heart ablaze for **HIS MISSION.**

The first of the two blue arrows has to do with being on mission. When you start to step out in obedience and become doers of the Word and not just hearers you realize this fundamental truth of the Kingdom: you never get more of Jesus than when you are giving Him away. You are never fuller than when you are pouring out.

Acts 1:8:

"But you will receive power when the Holy Spirit comes on you; and you will be my witnesses in Jerusalem, and in all Judea and Samaria, and to the ends of the earth".

It is a paradox of the Kingdom. The more you give, the more you get. It doesn't make sense! But that is how God designed it. We are called. I don't care if you are a single mom, a business man or woman, a college student, or a retiree... you have a call. Now I am not talking about vocational ministry, I am just talking about ministry. Period.

You are called to be witnesses. This wasn't just for the twelve disciples in the first century. This is for all disciples everywhere. If you are following Jesus then you are called to be His witness. Period. You are not just a recruit that sits on the sidelines; you are expected to play every down of every game!!

We are called to defend and love the marginalized. We are called to share the love and Gospel of Jesus with those who don't know Him. We are meant to be agents of change both individually and corporately... to bring heaven here on earth. Being on mission is not an option. It is a mandate for anyone who bears the name of Jesus.

There's a story told about a young soldier in the army of Alexander the Great who deserted his post and was tracked down and captured by Alexander's men. Normally deserters were quickly executed because of their disloyalty and disobedience to the king and his fellow soldiers, but according to this story, the young man was brought into the presence of the king. Alexander the Great demanded that the deserter tell him his name. The solider said, "I share the name of my king. My name is Alexander." And while King Alexander went on to pardon the deserter, he did not do so before saying, "Young man, you change your life, or you change your name."

If we aren't on mission, then we aren't fully following Jesus. If your life has not been changed to the degree that you are passionately joining Jesus in the mission and call He has given you, then you may want to rethink whether or not you really should go by the name "Christian."

Now if we are honest, there are times when we aren't focused on the mission and it gets hard. It gets lonely. We start to wonder if we are alone in this pursuit. But God never meant for us to be alone. We are made in the image of a triune God who is constantly in community with Himself.

We were made in His image. We were made to be in **COMMUNITY**.

This is not optional in our pursuit of and relationship with Jesus. The earliest followers of Jesus were devoted to fellowship because they had discovered that the way of Jesus cannot be lived alone.

Take a look at Acts 4:32-33:

Acts 4:32-33

"Now the full number of those who believed were of one heart and soul, and no one said that any of the things that belonged to him was his own, but they had everything in common. And with great power the apostles were giving their testimony to the resurrection of the Lord Jesus, and great grace was upon them all".

Don't miss the point; this was not communism. But it was absolutely an alternative to a life centered on self. And the results spoke for themselves. Power. Grace. There is nothing like fellowship. This is a challenge for many of us coming from a culture like ours. Individualism is the rule of the day. Narcissistic self-interest is unquestioned.

Devoting yourself to fellowship means refusing to settle for superficial community. You decide to take the risk and share life with other people growing in the same direction - toward God. True community is incredible. It's part of our being created in the image of God. When we are connected, we thrive. When we are disconnected, we wither.

In community, you find out who you really are in Christ through the loving voices of those who know you best. Gifts, talents, and passions get called out that you never knew you had. Community rejoices with you at your high points and carries you when you are down. Your spiritual blind spots get covered by friends who want the best for you and leaders called to oversee you.

It is in Christ we find out who we are and what we are made for, but it is often in community where this gets called out and confirmed. Sure, it's messy. It means you have to be selfless instead of selfish, and there is the possibility that you could get burned. But outside of community, we dry up. We sin. We fall short. The lone ranger can only go so far by himself. But in fellowship? Power and grace. You need other believers in your life.

Living in the green is not just a catchy phrase for us. It is the heartbeat and DNA of who we are. But this doesn't just happen on an individual level. True transformation happens when like-minded green disciples start taking this call seriously. Together. And the more we are being conformed and transformed into His image, the more we realize how much we need each other to be the body of Christ.

Living in the Green: As a Microchurch

I have led my own microchurch for over 5 years now and let's be honest: after two years or so, it was pretty predictable. We met together, had some fellowship time, worshipped, got in the Word, and broke off into accountability groups for prayer.

Now don't get me wrong: we were a good, healthy microchurch and there were some great God moments and good discipleship happening, but we all knew what was coming next. If I am honest, it became a little mundane. I knew I was in trouble when I started thinking to myself, "I wish we could mix it up a bit." If I, the microchurch leader, was thinking this, what was everyone else thinking?

So my microchurch and I came up with a new strategy of doing microchurch that fit with the "living in the green" discipleship strategy, because we believe all three aspects are needed to have balanced and holistic discipleship.

Instead of having the same, predictable schedule every week, we use what we have dubbed a **"Core 2, Green 2"** approach for our microchurch meetings. What this means is that for week 1 and 3 of any given month we follow a traditional microchurch model that includes time for fellowship, worship, studying the Word, and then prayer/accountability. We want these elements to remain a constant. That is a must. But for the other two weeks of the month, week 2 and 4, we have what we call a "Green night" (again, based off Greenhouse's discipleship model of worship, mission, community).

For these two nights, the goal is to have an activity that reflects these values of living in the green. The only rule is that week 4 must be different than week 2. For example, on week 2 if you do a community night, then week 4 would need to be a worship-focused night or a mission-focused night.

Here is an example of the monthly breakdown:

| | WEEK 1 | WEEK 2 | WEEK 3 | WEEK 4 |

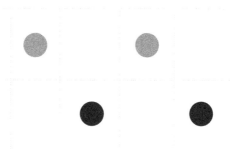

CORE NIGHT
Worship, Word, Accountability/ Prayer

GREEN NIGHT
Either Worship, Community, Mission Focused

For those of you who like practical ideas, here are some "Green night" examples of activities we have done:

Worship Focus	Night of worship where we all spent the entire evening worshiping, night of intercessory prayer focused on a need in the group, prophecy night where we did a teaching on prophecy and then prophesied over one another, etc.
Community Focus	Pot luck (that is all we did that night, just hanging out in community), game nights (spades tournament, ultimate frisbee, etc.), we went out to dinner with our tiny groups and had an accountability night, etc.
Mission Focus	Prayer walked the neighborhood, evangelism, invite nights (everyone went out and invited others to a Bring weekend), service projects, etc.

I want to be clear here: **this model is not the only way to do this,** but we want you asking God how to keep your microchurch green. If your microchurch is deficient in any of these three areas, your disciples will be deficient as well. It is important that you leverage your microchurch to promote and produce green discipleship.

Reflection Questions:
Helping your Microchurch stay green

As a leader, which of the three aspects of living in the green are you most passionate about? Which one is the hardest for you to live out?

How can you help cultivate the aspect of green living that is the hardest for you in the context of your microchurch?

Of the three elements of living in the green, which one does your microchurch lean most heavily to?

Are you a worshiping MC or do you all just love to hang out in community? Or are you a bunch of evangelists and activists that just want to go do stuff all the time?

Which of the three elements of living in the green does your microchurch neglect the most?

Are you a great God-loving community that doesn't do anything outside of your own little group? Are you a vibrant community that outreaches all the time but doesn't really have God in the center of it?

What are some ways you can ensure that your microchurch is getting a healthy mix of all three elements of living in the green?

Is your microchurch too churchy for an unchurched person to want to come? Why or why not?

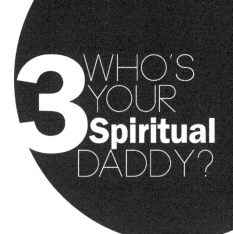

3 WHO'S YOUR Spiritual DADDY?

My parents got divorced when I was eleven years old. I will never forget the day my dad came into my room and was tucking me in that night. He was running his hand through my hair as he usually did when he was home to say goodnight. He was looking at me with a smile but there was deep sorrow underneath his smile that I picked up on, even as an eleven year old. He proceeded to tell me that he was going to have to go away for awhile. In fact, he told me that he actually would never live with my mom again. He assured me it wasn't anything I did and that he still loved me and we would still spend time together. Although I didn't fully understand what was going on at the time, I did know that things would never be the same. And it was true: things were never the same.

There were a lot of things my dad did right. There were a lot of things my dad did wrong. There were a lot of things I learned from him, but there were a lot of things I did not learn from him because the context wasn't the same after he left.

Now that I'm a dad and continue to give myself to following as closely to Jesus as I can, and one of my most desperate desires is that my family loves the Lord with all their heart, soul, mind and strength. More than anything I want my daughter Alethea to be a strong woman of God and I am resolved to do everything in my power to ensure that she grows up in an environment where she sees her father and mother living out the faith that we hold so dear. I want her to be able to see how a disciple lives, loves, celebrates, mourns, repents... to see every element of discipleship. And I am not going to outsource that.

Why? Alethea has one father here on earth, and it is my duty, my privilege, and my delight to raise her in the ways of the Lord. Even though I am so excited at the prospect of some of the amazing pastors on our staff being teachers and instructors in Alethea's life, she only has one father. I am her father. And despite the fact that we have unbelievable teaching pastors and staff here at the Greenhouse Church, no one can take my place as her father or diminish the influence that I have in her life. No one.

If anyone understood this fatherly desire to ensure his children were brought up in the ways of the Lord, albeit his spiritual children, it was Paul. First Corinthians 4:15-17 says, "Even if you had ten thousand instructors in Christ, you do not have many fathers, for in Christ Jesus I became your father through the gospel. Therefore I urge you to imitate me. For this reason I have sent to you Timothy, my son whom I love, who is faithful in the Lord. He will remind you of my way of life in Christ Jesus, which agrees with what I teach everywhere in every church."

There is a difference between good teachers and spiritual fathers and mothers. Paul was one of the most prolific disciples, church planters, and disciple makers of all time. Even secular sources such as TIME magazine rank him as one of the most influential people in all of history.

His reach goes throughout the world and continues to impact billions of people in our generation. Paul's legacy is unprecedented in any faith history. And there is a reason for that. Paul viewed his faith and discipleship through a very unique and world changing lens which separated him from others in the early church and even the church today. There were specific things Paul did that allowed him to be as successful as he was in regard to church planting and disciple making and 1st Corinthians 5:15-17 really highlights this unique angle of the apostle Paul.

Did you have siblings growing up? If so, did you have younger siblings that would drive you crazy by copying everything you did? When you were starting to get mad at them you would say something like, "Don't you touch my stuff!" and then your little brother or sister would blatantly mock and mimic you by saying in a high pitch, annoying voice, "Don't you touch my stuff!" which would enrage you more. And then you'd say, "I'm serious!" and in their most mocking tone they would repeat, "I'm serious!" and they just kept doing everything you did and saying everything you said until you would punch them... and then you got in trouble!

What you didn't know was that your annoying little sibling was unlocking the keys of disciple making right before your eyes. Nowhere do you see Paul settling with Timothy just being a good disciple, or Apollos just doing well and taking care of his family. Nope. Paul always had a vision that saw generations of disciples beyond the person he was talking to. And what your annoying little brother or sister got right was the idea of intimate imitation.

We need microchurch leaders in the church who are living lives worth imitating and who then allow others to live life with them in a way that affords them opportunities to imitate what they see.

Let me repeat that passage:

> **I Corinthians 4:15-17**
>
> "Even if you had ten thousand instructors in Christ, you do not have many fathers, for in Christ Jesus I became your father through the gospel. Therefore I urge you to imitate me. For this reason I have sent to you Timothy, my son whom I love, who is faithful in the Lord. He will remind you of my way of life in Christ Jesus, which agrees with what I teach everywhere in every church."

Paul was not just a teacher; he was a spiritual father. And Paul wasn't looking to reproduce good teachers; he wanted to reproduce himself, more specifically other spiritual fathers and mothers. Friends, we have enough teachers of the Word, good teachers at that, to fill your podcasts for the rest of your life... literally. You could listen to Francis Chan, John Piper, Matt Chandler, David Platt, TD Jakes, and Mike Patz for the rest of your life and still not be a green disciple, much less a disciple maker. Teachers are not what we are lacking in the church. We are lacking spiritual fathers and mothers. People that Christians can look to, live life with, see the good and the bad, and learn how to imitate.

Paul's words "Therefore I urge you to imitate me," scare Christians today and we aren't even sure if we want to say this anymore. If that is the case, then your discipleship legacy will die with you. It will not make it past your spiritual generation.

Paul, however, had a vision of a discipleship legacy that went far beyond himself or the people he was discipling and with whom he was in community. Throughout the New Testament he makes radical calls to his disciples, like this statement in II Timothy 2:2, "And the things you heard me say in the presence of many witnesses entrust to reliable men who will be qualified to teach others." Paul had a vision for not only Timothy, but for the disciples of Timothy and the disciples of Timothy's disciples. When Paul spoke he was looking four generations into the future, desperate to ensure that discipleship continued well beyond the person he was speaking to at the moment.

So I need you to answer one of the most critical questions you can ask yourself as a microchurch leader:

Is your vision to simply lead a microchurch, or to change the world by making disciple makers?

Are you simply going to give a lesson each week, or are you going to be peering into the next four generations of disciples that you are intending to make?

Are you going to give correct instruction, or are you going to be a spiritual father or mother?

Teachers simply teach and go home, hoping that something sticks. But fathers and mothers are much more invested. Fathers and mothers willingly take the time and effort to help their children grow up. A good mother, a good father, is one that is there for their child and helps them grow up to become the man or woman they are called to be.

And Paul was so sure of himself and the disciples he made that he could say, "For this reason I have sent to you Timothy, my son whom I love, who is faithful in the Lord. He will remind you of my way of life in Christ Jesus, which agrees with what I teach everywhere in every church," (I Corinthians 4:17) and be fully confident that as long as Timothy was there, the believers would get everything Paul had to offer.

Microchurch leaders, are you that confident about the people in your microchurch? If you couldn't show up somewhere, could you just as easily send your apprentices and microchurch members and repeat what Paul said in verse 17?

That can be a daunting question, but the last thing I want this to be is a condemnation trip. That is not what I am hoping will happen when you read this chapter. But I pray this question is one that you have a desperate kingdom desire to be able to answer in the affirmative. That's why you're reading this book; you want to give your life for the Gospel and make it count. You want to make it count. You don't want to waste your life on stupid things that don't matter, but you want to sow and reap in eternity. That's why you have responded to the call to become a microchurch leader. And that is why we are so thankful for you!

Because friends, and I know you can relate, I don't JUST want teachers to be leading our microchurches. I don't JUST want information disseminated. I don't JUST want people to come to a microchurch to consume like a baby bird that never leaves the nest. No, because that is not the call of Jesus. Jesus calls us to make disciples who are going to make disciples. And I want you to have the proper training and the tools to do just that!

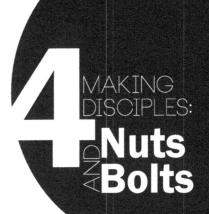

4 MAKING DISCIPLES: **Nuts AND Bolts**

The microchurch staff has been brainstorming and talking about discipleship: what effective discipleship looks like, how we got discipled, what works, what doesn't, how to do it well and we came up with this section as a primer for this disciple making conversation. This is not a step 1-10 discipleship model, but is more like a foundational framework for discipleship to help you move from simply teaching a microchurch to becoming spiritual fathers and mothers who have a great and fulfilling run as a microchurch leader making some radical disciples.

This is our version of training wheels for discipleship. Are you already an effective disciple maker? Great. Keep doing what you are doing! We hope this helps sharpen your skills. But if you are new to this concept of making disciples who make disciples, then we really want you to digest this material and start putting it into practice. We don't just want microchurch leaders, we want spiritual fathers and mothers and we want to show you the way to do that if you do not already know how.

I am convinced that with just a little bit of intentionality in what you do already, you can easily become an effective disciple maker. You are already a strong disciple: now it is time to move into the realm of disciple making. Most of you already meet with people throughout the week, but you may just need to be strategic about the conversations you're having and make sure they are "green" and focused on discipleship.

Many of you have a heart for kingdom activity, and we want to make sure you have a plan and a way to live it out so that you know you are making disciples. Most of you, by simply bringing someone along when you are seeking the Lord, memorizing Scripture, witnessing, etc. would be radical disciple makers.

The key in all of this is being INTENTIONAL!

So what does it mean to make a disciple? That is a great question that we hope to help you answer. While we don't believe there is just one way to disciple someone, we do think there are a few aspects of discipleship that cannot be overlooked if our aim is to truly help ordinary people become passionate followers of Jesus Christ:

KEY ELEMENTS OF A DISCIPLESHIP MODEL

Start and End Date
Small Core, Strong Commitment
Green Emphasis
Scripture Memorization
Accountability
Seeking the Lord (Together)
Multiple Touches a Week
Disciples Who Make Disciples

START AND END DATE

Nothing is worse than miscommunication or unmet expectations. While there are some instances where discipleship happens over a lifetime, the majority of the time discipleship is done in seasons.

Like Jesus and his few years with the disciples or Paul raising up elders in a city for a few months and then leaving, discipleship happens for a period of time and then the disciple is expected to become the disciple maker.

This model of discipleship has a clear beginning and end and aims to conclude after a span of 12 months. At the end of this time, ideally the person being discipled is now ready to become a disciple maker too. (This doesn't mean you still won't stay in touch or have the occasional conversation; it simply means that you are focusing your discipleship energies on a new set of up and coming disciples.)

SMALL CORE, STRONG COMMITMENT

If you as a disciple maker are willing to give your attention, energy, and time to people you are discipling, then you should expect the same kind of commitment from them. Have them commit to meeting weekly and making that time a priority.

Strong discipleship happens within the context of a small core. Jesus had 12 disciples, but spent focused time with 3. Focus this discipleship time on 2-4 people to maximize your focus and efforts.

GREEN EMPHASIS

We want our disciples to be green: worshipping, on mission, and in community. While we do give a variety of options for study materials to use with the people you are discipling, one non-negotiable is that the resources you select are green, meaning they focus on God and living a lifestyle of worship (spiritual disciplines, theology, etc.), community (authenticity, accountability, etc.) and mission (evangelism, justice, generosity, etc.) We want green disciples!

SCRIPTURE MEMORIZATION

Man does not live on bread alone, but on every Word that comes from the mouth of God. We believe this and believe that disciples need to have not only a daily intake of the Word, but the Word written on their hearts. Scripture memorization is a way to ensure the Word is permeating our worldviews, beliefs, and lifestyles at the deepest level.

ACCOUNTABILITY

The way of Jesus is one of learning and doing, not just listening to the lectures of our teachers. We expect ongoing spiritual formation to take place in every believer's life and we recognize that this takes place in the midst of everyday activities, which leads to a life of wholeness and reproduction. Discipleship happens when real people make face-to-face and heart-to-heart contact with each other.

SEEKING THE LORD (TOGETHER)

Imitation is embedded in us biologically and theologically. We imitate and learn from those closest to us, and spiritual disciplines such as prayer and Bible study are no exception. People need to see mature believers praying, interceding, and interacting with the Word. Having space each week to learn and sharpen one another spiritually is a huge part of becoming a strong disciple

MULTIPLE TOUCHES A WEEK

Discipleship is caught, not taught. It is hard to condense true discipleship into a once a week classroom style meeting. Discipleship truly takes place when life is lived together and new disciples are able to watch it lived out. Watching a disciple maker live a green lifestyle speaks volumes, and that can't just happen once a week. Pray together, eat together, talk about the Bible together, witness together, party together... let your disciple see every aspect of your life!

DISCIPLES WHO MAKE DISCIPLES

Disciples are not disciples if they are not reproducing other disciples. Part of the commitment of discipleship is that the person being poured into is willing to make the commitment to in turn pour into someone else. This isn't optional. We don't want to transfer knowledge; we want what is learned put into practice and thus fulfill the command to go and make disciples...

Do What You are Already Doing: Sample Discipleship Schedule

Let's say Frank is a microchurch leader and his microchurch meets on Tuesday nights. Here is an example of how he could incorporate all of the things we just reviewed by only adding one hour meeting to his weekly schedule.

SUNDAY LUNCH AFTER CHURCH
Meet at a restaurant <u>after church</u> and go over Scripture memorization for the week, do accountability, and review an aspect of the green curriculum while sharing a meal.

TUESDAY NIGHT
<u>Have disciples come early</u> and touch base with Frank about MC, pray with them, and then actively participate and help lead microchurch.

THURSDAY MORNING
Have disciples join him in seeking the Lord from <u>7:00 – 8:00 am</u> at a specific location (his house, the church, a park, etc.).

LOOK FAMILIAR? IS THIS WHAT YOU ALREADY DO THROUGHOUT YOUR WEEK? Exactly. The most effective disciple makers bring people along on things they are already doing.

As a microchurch leader, you are already going to be at microchurch, so you don't have to add anything to your schedule. Just be more intentional about getting them actively involved in helping you pray for and lead the microchurch. If you are a leader or are discipling others you are already doing that as well. The only thing added to your weekly schedule is a one-time meeting to sharpen one another through the Word, accountability, and the curriculum. This can be done any time throughout the week, after church, at lunchtime during the week, one evening, one morning a week... whatever works for you and the people you are discipling.

THE GOAL IS TO LIVE LIFE WITH ONE ANOTHER AND SHOW THEM WHAT A GREEN LIFESTYLE LOOKS LIKE. LET THEM FOLLOW YOU AS YOU FOLLOW CHRIST!

DON'T get caught up in keeping a checklist. Stay flexible and let the Holy Spirit fill the gaps!! If you think that discipleship is going to fit perfectly into your life, think again. Be ready for untimely calls, texts, and for unscheduled meetings! It is part of living life with people. It is also important how you respond because even in these moments discipleship is taking place! Discipleship is caught, not taught.

RECAP

1. 12 MONTH COMMITMENT

2. NO MORE THAN 2-4 PEOPLE

3. MULTIPLE TOUCHES WEEKLY (MC, SEEKING THE LORD, & OTHER TIME(S)

4. EXPECT THE PEOPLE YOU DISCIPLE WILL DISCIPLE OTHERS.

RESOURCES

We at Greenhouse have worked hard to create a discipleship curriculum that would help you make disciples who can then use that same resource to go and make disciples themselves. It is called "The Green Book" and we are excited to have that available for you. It goes over our leadership fluencies and has Scripture to memorize together, questions to ask the people you are discipling after each section, and is a great primer and tool for discipleship conversations. You can get a copy on amazon.com if you put "green disciple" in the search bar or talk to a Greenhouse staff member and they can get you a copy if they are available at the church!

Reflection Questions:
Making disciples (who make disciples)

What would you say are some key characteristics of a spiritual father/mother? What separates them from a good teacher for example?

What is holding you back from being a spiritual mom or dad?

What can you do to reorient your life around the Great Commission?

Do you feel confident saying "Follow me as I follow Christ?"

Why or why not? If not, explain how you are going to remedy that!

What elements of making disciples excite you and will be easy?

What will be the most difficult? How will you overcome those obstacles?

How do you make disciples who are going to make other disciples? How do you get that DNA in them?

THE 2-2-2 PRINCIPLE

2nd Timothy 2:2

"And the things you have heard me say in the presence of many witnesses, entrust to reliable men who will also be qualified to teach others."

I am convinced that Paul was a genius. A Spirit-led, Spirit-filled genius. The man knew what he was doing. I am also convinced that if we want to have any sort of lasting legacy in our life or walk with Jesus, we need to heed Paul's strategy.

Paul speaks of reproducing leaders into the fourth generation:

→ *PAUL* (1st generation)

　→ instructs *TIMOTHY* (2nd generation)

　　→ to invest in *"RELIABLE MEN"* (3rd generation)

　　　→ who will also be qualified to *TEACH OTHERS* (4th generation)

Let that settle in your soul for a second. When we examine this idea of apprenticeship, we are not talking about finding people to help us do tasks more effectively. We're not talking about finding a decent replacement so if we want to move on to other things someone can step in. We are talking about reproducing godly leaders so that the mission and microchurch won't die with us but is carried on to future generations!

If I sound redundant, please forgive me, but I hope by now you have been able to pick up on our microchurch DNA. There are really two things that I want burned into your spirit when it comes to leading a microchurch. There are two non-neogtiables for our microchurch leaders to fully understand, embrace, and implement. Two things that every microchurch leader should be doing and pursuing:

1. Making green disciples

2. Multiplying microchurches by reproducing apprentices.

These are the two things that you should always be aspiring to do as a microchurch leader. Microchurches without discipleship are not okay. The point of microchurches is to facilitate discipleship, not to have another weekly church meeting.

IF YOU MAKE DISCIPLES, YOU ALWAYS GET THE CHURCH. BUT IF YOU SIMPLY HAVE A CHURCH MEETING, YOU RARELY GET DISCIPLES.[1]

A good discipleship thought from Mike Breen.

The same is also true in a microchurch setting. This means discipleship, the art of reproducing green disciples, should always be the focal point and center of everything you do as a microchurch leader. Everything you do should be centered around making green disciples and moving you towards multiplication. Period.

This is how it has been done throughout the entirety of the New Testament, but we get an up close and personal model of this especially in the lives and ministries of Jesus and Paul. Jesus functionally had a microchurch of twelve disciples, but He focused extra time and attention on what I call His three apprentices: James, Peter and John who all became foundational pillars of the early church. Paul also was constantly raising up apprentices and launching them out to plant churches, oversee church plants, and have them do to others what Paul did for them.

Everywhere Jesus and Paul went, they left apprentices, disciples, and leaders in their wake. It was a natural by-product of their ministry; apprentices were raised up to step into leadership positions. And because of this, disciples learned how to make disciples who planted churches, and those churches planted other churches that multiplied everywhere in the known world.

And we want to do exactly what Paul did: raise up apprentices who are going to raise up disciples and plant churches and microchurches throughout the known world. So this begs the question: Why was Paul so effective in ministry, as a church planter and as a spiritual father? Because he discipled people well. He was able to say things like "Follow me as I follow Christ," and that had weight and meaning.

Are you confident enough to say that? Does your life reflect that? If not, I hope you are tweaking it, because as a leader you need to have that kind of confidence in your walk... while at the same time realizing that in the Kingdom, this simply means you have an ever-increasing dependency on the Lord for your confidence. Your confidence has to be a Christ-in-you confidence, not just self-confidence. And there's a big difference.

Jesus does the transformation in you and in the people you disciple, but you facilitate that process as a microchurch leader and a disciple maker. No one accidentally creates disciples. No one says, "Oh my gosh, I accidentally made a disciple! I don't know how that happened!" No, you know how it happened because you were radically invested in that process. Discipleship and raising up an apprentice in your microchurch are focused pursuits that don't happen if you are not intentional.

Raising Apprentices in Your Microchurch: What to Look For

Apprenticing is discipleship with a leadership focus. Jesus had three apprentices: James, Peter, and John. These were the guys that led the early church after His ascension. Not that the other disciples didn't play a part, but these were the guys Jesus poured the most into and these were the guys who stepped into leadership after he was gone. Jesus, Paul and any other successful leader in the church knew the importance of having an apprentice and how to equip them to succeed, and I want to break this down for you on an extremely practical level.

The first thing you have to do if you want to raise up apprentices in your microchurch is determine who the leaders in your microchurch are. This seems like a ridiculously obvious statement, but you would be amazed at how many leaders don't get this step right. And I'll be honest; it is a lot harder than you might think. I see leaders pouring into the wrong people all the time. So you need to know what characteristics to look for in an apprentice and then invest in those people.

I always look for three things in an apprentice: I go after those who are **hungry, faithful, and fruitful**. I don't necessarily go after the most mature people in my microchurch or the ones I think would be the best leaders based on what others have told me. Talk to any leader and they will tell you that they have been burned too many times by that. I strictly go after the hungry, faithful, and fruitful.

This is what Jesus did. He always had a crowd around Him. But when the crowd got too big, what did Jesus do? He would say ridiculously hard statements and freak people out to try to get them to go away! He would say things like, "If you want to follow Me, you have to eat My flesh and drink My blood." Jesus was weeding out those who were just there for the free fish and bread and to gawk at the miracles. He was seeing who was really committed. And when the crowd left, Jesus turned to His disciples and said, "Are you going to leave, too?" The disciples were probably confused by all of this, but Jesus was testing their commitment. He wanted to see if the disciples were hungry for the things of God and were faithful to stick with Him, even when it got tough.

And this is what I look for in my microchurch: people who fit this bill. So I intentionally do things to subtly and not so subtly test the faithfulness, hunger, and fruitfulness of potential leaders. I never dub anyone an apprentice until they have consistently proven themselves in these three areas.

For example, my microchurch meets on a Tuesday night. Every Thursday for the past year I have invited everyone from my microchurch via a weekly email or text to come pray with me on Thursday mornings. I am already going to be seeking the Lord, and with a little bit of intentionality, I am able to turn that into a weekly discipleship moment. Now I am very aware of the people who show up because for me, this is an apprenticeship test. People who are hungry for the things of God show up at 6 am or 7 am on Thursday mornings to pray. Period. They are hungry for Jesus.

A few years ago, before I did Thursday morning prayer, I had microchurch prayer on Friday mornings and for most of the year, only one guy came. One guy. You may think that was a bust: if you have a MC of 25 people and only one guy shows up? Yikes! But that's not true if you have eyes to see. It was a huge win because it showed me who my next apprentice was. It showed he was utterly faithful and very hungry.

I have a guy I am currently discipling who meets for Thursday morning prayer. He came in sleepy one morning and I asked what was going on. He said he couldn't really fall asleep the night before and only got two hours of sleep. *But he was still there at 6 am!!!*

Faithful. Hungry.

Not only are people learning how to pray, hear from God, and sharpen their devotional time, but they are proving themselves as potential apprentices.

I realize that some people can't make it in the mornings due to family or job restrictions. But you can do a myriad of things that will reveal to you the hunger, faithfulness, and fruitfulness of a potential apprentice.

One thing I try to do is find out the giftings of a potential leader and see how well they flow in that gift. Last year I had a guy named Gram who showed leadership potential in my microchurch. He was always striking up conversations with new people, getting their numbers, and meeting them outside of microchurch.

So I put him to test.

Since I couldn't keep up with everyone from my microchurch personally, I delegated four guys to him and asked if he would keep up with them throughout the week. Every week I would ask about the guys and he would have talked to or met with all of them. When I talked to those four guys, they would rave about how good Gram was at being there for them.

Faithfulness. Fruitfulness.

Gram ended up multiplying out of my microchurch and starting a vibrant one of his own.

So microchurch leaders, potential leaders, here's the thing. Go after the hungry, faithful, and fruitful... don't waste your time on people who don't exhibit these qualities. Spend the majority of your time reproducing yourself into others who will in turn reproduce themselves into others as well! 2nd Timothy 2:2 says "Entrust to reliable men.... RELIABLE MEN, who will be qualified to teach others." Paul makes an important stipulation: qualified to teach others.

Jesus gave the very famous parable of the soil. Now he was talking about the Gospel and salvation, but this definitely works for discipleship and apprenticeship as well. Basically Jesus says only one in four people are good soil, but that good soil is going to produce a 30, 60,or 100 fold crop! Let me put it another way. Let's say you had $1,000 to invest and after surveying the stock options, there were four stocks to choose from: three seemed decent, but their returns were erratic, while another stock could yield you 3,000% – 10,000% profit. Where would you put your money? You'd better believe I'm putting my money in a 10,000% return! Are you crazy? This is a no brainer!!

We have something here that is far more valuable than money... we are dealing with disciples who make disciples, thus ensuring that discipleship will continue even when we are gone. Bottom line: Go after those who want it and will yield a good discipleship crop!

John Wesley said, "Go to those who want you and go most to those who want you the most."

There was a guy in my microchurch who was a solid disciple.

He loved the Lord, was growing, made great contributions at microchurch; I thought he had apprentice written all over him.

He even came to me and asked if I would disciple him, and I said, "Definitely!" I mean, I couldn't ask for a better set-up, so I invited him to meet me on Thursday morning for prayer. He told me he couldn't make it. When I asked why, he told me he had class in the morning. When I asked what time, he told me 9:00 am. (I pray with my microchurch from 6:00-8:00 am, so I was confused as to why he couldn't make it.) Long story short, he was not willing to make the commitment to get up early and come pray.

This doesn't mean he was a bad disciple or that he didn't love Jesus, but if he was not willing to at least try to make it on Thursday morning because he didn't want to go to bed early, then I was not going to coddle this guy. I had other people in my microchurch who were so hungry that they were willing to come at 6 am even if they went to bed at 3:30 am! You see what I am getting at here? Your time as a leader is valuable and you shouldn't waste it on people who aren't going to show up and that you are going to have to chase all the time.

Now don't get me wrong; just because someone is not a morning person doesn't mean they are somehow less of a disciple or that if you don't wake up early to pray then you are a worthless leader. But for me, this was a test. If he would have even told me, "Hey man, I am not a morning person, so could we meet up at night instead?" it would have been a different story. That would have showed hunger and a desire to go the extra mile and I could have worked with that. The bottom line remains: go after the hungry, the faithful, and the fruitful.

Here are some good questions to help you discern potential apprentices:

HUNGRY

Do they have a Jesus centered life? Is Jesus permeating his/her marriage, finances, parenting, school, work, etc?

Do you see a strong desire to grow in their relationship with Jesus? Do they spend daily time with the Lord in the secret place?

Are they moving closer to Jesus or farther away? Is there a long devotion in the same direction?

(They don't have to have been following Jesus for five years to be a good microchurch leader... but you can be following Jesus for five years and not be a good leader)

FAITHFUL

Are they radically commited to your microchurch? Would you consider them one of your core members?

Do they show a desire to help and assist you in aspects of your microchurch, or do they leave that for others to do?

Do they follow through when you ask them to do things?

FRUITFUL

Do others show a willingess to follow him/her? If he/she started something, do you think others would follow? Why or why not?

When they lead/teach/set up an event, does it go well? Bear fruit?

Would they pass the "parking lot test"? (When you see the potential apprentice's car in the parking lot as you pull in, is your initial reaction one of excitement to see them, or do you hope you'll be able to avoid them?) This is a chemistry question: when this person walks into the room, how do people feel? Leadership is not solely about the positional title, it is about the relationship as well!

6 DELE GATION AND APPREN TICE SHIP

THE POWER OF THE D WORD

I am about to give you the best word a leader could ever hear. Write this word down, circle it, highlight it, star it, draw hearts around it if you're a girl because this is going to be your best friend as a leader. This is one of the main leadership principles that separates multiplying microchurches from good Bible studies. The word is: DELEGATE. Now pick up this book and smell it. Mmm, delegation even smells good. This is another absolutely critical key to effectively raising up and reproducing apprentices.

FACT: The best microchurch leaders never lead.

They are out of the leadership equation. The best leaders could simply stop coming to microchurch one week and never return because they have taught their microchurch to be self-sufficient. Success for me as a microchurch leader is when an evening could have gone on without a hitch even if I wasn't there. My goal every time I get together with my microchurch is for everything to be delegated to others.

It is a win when you are not needed as a leader anymore.

Now I'm not going to lie: delegation was really hard for me at first. I have a high value on excellence and I want everything done perfectly. I have a vision for it and I want things executed to the "T". So delegating is hard because people don't always do it the way I want it done. But by delegating, I am giving others an opportunity to learn how to lead. And although it may not always be the way I would have done it, sometimes it turns out even better. At other times when things I have delegated have turned out messy, I remind myself that the goal is not to have a perfect meeting, but to equip disciples, and these situations become great learning opportunities and discipleship moments.

The way to delegate to an apprentice is a three-fold strategy:

① DELEGATE TO PEOPLE'S STRENGTHS AND GIFTINGS

Find out what their strengths are. What do they love to do? Are they administratively minded? Are they a shepherd? A teacher? An evangelist? Let them lead in these areas. Don't ask an introverted administrator to lead an evangelism outreach and then get mad at them when the evening tanks! If they are clueless, help them get in touch with their giftings and let them accrue a few wins under the belt in their area of passion and expertise. Let teachers lead the discussion for the night. Allow the shepherds to plan events and do follow up with people. Give people with the gift of hospitality an opportunity to open up their homes to the microchurch or bake for microchurch that week.

It is important for them to realize their strengths and then learn how to serve from those strengths. A good leadership principle is that you are not supposed to work on your weaknesses, but lead from your strengths. Most people have not figured out what their strengths are so it is your job to help them figure that out, which leads to our next step.

2. CALL OUT PEOPLE'S GIFTINGS: "I C N U"

This is how every conversation that has to do with delegation should start. It is one of the most important and impactful parts of delegation, because the question people most want answered is not, "What is in it for me?" The real question is, "Why me? Why did you choose me instead of someone else?"

If you simply say to someone, "Hey, I need someone to follow up with those guys. Can you do it?", they might. But listen to how the conversation shifts when you add the ICNU (I See in You) element to it. I will use Gram, who multiplied out of my microchurch as an example.

"Hey Gram, I've been watching you for awhile in microchurch now. You didn't know it, but I have been, and I have been blown away by how radical a shepherd you are. I mean, it is written all over you. Bro, you just bless people because your heart is for them. It is so natural for you that I bet you don't even realize you are doing it. The way you talk with people, the way you welcome newcomers and are always the first one to say hello, how you always make sure they never sit alone, it means the world to that person. And the way you follow up with everyone throughout the week... not everyone does that! It's a gift, man, and the Lord has wired you to radically impact people with that gift.

I'll be honest; I could use some help shepherding some of these guys in microchurch. Do you think you could cover four guys and do what you already love doing? Follow up with them, love on them, and be there for them? It would be a huge help and a huge blessing to these guys, to me, and to our microchurch, if you would be willing to take them under your wing. What do you say?"

Notice the difference there? When you add the ICNU element it is a game changer. You are validating the person and helping reveal to them the Lord's unique design for them. It is a life-giving conversation and makes a huge investment in the life of your potential apprentice. Even if they don't end up being your apprentice, this is still a vital exercise to do as a leader. Call out the gifts that God has given them!

③ ACTIVATE THE GIFT!

This is the third and final step to delegation. Give them things to do! Help them get in touch with their gifts, call those gifts out in them, and then let them get their hands dirty in helping with the microchurch. Good leaders will purposefully seek people who can supplement their weakness as a leader. So if you are a strong shepherd with terrible admin skills, find an administratively minded person to help with weekly emails, attendance, etc. If you are a teacher and all you want to do is get in the Word, make sure you are activating the evangelist in your microchurch to ensure you stay green and stay on mission. If you are an apostle and all you want is new stuff, make sure you have a shepherd who will take care of the people while you are off on your next new thing.

Delegation is a way to ensure your microchruch is well rounded but also a way to raise up apprentices after you've observed who is hungry, faithful, and fruitful with what you delegate. Remember that your primary purpose as a leader is NOT to have a good, warm, fuzzy microchurch. Your primary purpose is to make green disciples and multiply your microchurch so that we have more venues for discipleship taking place and more opportunities for the Lord to add to your number daily those who are being saved.

Life on Life:
Get out of the classroom!

Once you have delegation going on in your microchurch and have an eye for the hungry, faithful and fruitful, you are now ready to tap your apprentices on the shoulder and take them under your wing.

There are many different ways to apprentice someone, but the most effective way is to simply let them into your life. If the only time you are meeting with your apprentice is during your microchurch, that is not sufficient. Discipleship is caught, not taught, so the more they are around you the better!

Have them join you in what you are already doing. People don't need more classroom style discipleship. Teach them as you go. One of the biggest misnomers is that discipleship means you have to add extra meetings to your life. You don't need to do that. Simply bring them along with what you are already doing. If you are already praying in the mornings, invite them to do that with you.

If you are having dinner with your family, once a week invite them to come. If you are following up with people from microchurch, have them join you. If you grocery shopping, bring them along to get groceries with you!! Exposure is key to discipleship and raising up effective apprentices.

Mike Breen talks about exposure and how that played into Jesus' apprenticeship model: "Jesus had what many scholars call his 'Retreat Ministry,' a period of time that was dedicated completely to the disciples, when he retreated to places the crowds would never follow, when the disciples could be immersed in relationship and have complete access to him. Here's the interesting thing: Most people think that at least eighteen months of Jesus' public ministry was this time. That means at least half of his time was spent with these twelve guys. He believed so powerfully in discipleship that he basically put all of his eggs into that basket. (It's worth noting that it paid off.)"

 There is something about exposure that solidifies discipleship like nothing else does. It's the way Jesus did it so I think we need to take this seriously.

There are two guys who I am discipling right now, and I see Kurt and Brad at least four times a week: Tuesday morning prayer, Tuesday night microchurch, Thursday morning prayer and discipleship, and Sunday nights at Leadership Pipeline. I am with these guys a minimum of at least 6-8 hours a week. Why? Because I want them to see the rhythm of life and leadership that I have. I want them to experience time with the Lord with me. I want them to have everything they need to be strong disciple makers themselves. I want them to follow me as I follow Christ. You might think, "Eight hours? That's a lot!"

[1] Breen, Mike. Building a Discipleship Culture.

It might sound like a lot, but I am simply bringing them along to things I am already doing. Now if you are saying to yourself, "Oh, I am way too busy for that!", I would strongly disagree.

You just need to figure out where there can be overlap in your schedule to bring them along. Don't add extra meetings. Have your lunches with your disciples.Go to church together and then have lunch with them afterwards with you and your family. Seek the Lord together. Bring them to your kids' sporting events. Work out with them. Run errands together. You can do it if you are intentional, and it will become second nature.

Discipleship isn't optional as a follower of Christ. It is the Great Commission, not the Great Suggestion.

Now this doesn't mean that you have to spend 6-8 hours a week with someone to be a good disciple maker. Kurt and Brad are single, fresh out of college, and don't have families, so they can flex more time than the average person. The underlying point here is that you spend as much time as you can with the people you are discipling! Think outside the box and let them be a part of your life in any way that you can make happen!

Brad, Kurt and I also hang out outside of our four weekly meetings (which are things I am already doing), because we are friends. I have simply invited them into the rhythm of my life and they are always welcome to more of it if they want. We go out to breakfast or dinner every now and then, as well, but these are spur of the moment occurrences.

I want to be clear: we are not mass-producing discipleship robots; we are living life with future disciple makers that we care about and love. Like Paul, we should have this type of attitude with the people we are apprenticing: "Because we loved you so much, we were delighted to share with you not only the gospel of God but our lives as well" (I Thessalonians 2:8). People need to see and experience this type of discipleship so they can pass it on to the next generation of disciple makers.

Historically, in agrarian culture this type of learn as-you-go paradigm was common practice even in farming techniques: "When it was time to plant the crops, you had to make sure the fields were plowed. The massive, wooden plows were quite heavy, and usually only a team of oxen was able to drag the plow through the field, tilling and preparing the soil for the seed that would come next. Obviously, the team of oxen was pulling the plow together and was held together by a yoke that bridled them. What these farmers did was partner a young, very energetic ox with a much older, seasoned ox that had plowed the fields for many seasons. The farmers found that the younger ox would push quite hard at the beginning of the day, using up all of his energy and would have nothing left for the second half of the day. Remember, we're talking eleven-to twelve-hour work days.

However, when bridled with an older, more experienced ox, the younger ox would be forced to learn the rhythm and pace of the day. He couldn't run ahead because he was bridled to the older ox. And so, eventually, the young ox learned the best rhythm from the older ox so he could last for the whole day and was able to keep an even, sustained pace. The rhythms of life were passed from one to the other. Eventually, the younger ox would grow older, have more seasons under his metaphorical belt and would then be paired with a new, younger ox, and the cycle would continue."

We want apprentices yoked with healthy leaders who have good leadership rhythms. This won't fully happen until you let them in to your life and leadership rhythm.

Below is a cursory list of things I have done with my apprentices that can be done "on the go" as a way to disciple them:

Spend time seeking the Lord together.

Teach them to know the Word through reading Scripture together and dialoguing about it.

Play sports with them and talk about leadership and teamwork .

Memorize Scripture together and teaching them to apply it.

Pray for your microchurch together.

Delegate small aspects of the microchurch... then give them more and more until they are leading the entire microchurch and can lead it all.

Breen, Mike. Building a Discipleship Culture.

Pray for microchurch members together.

Constantly talk through living in the green and how that applies when we are at microchurch, at work, in the grocery store, etc.

Have them contact members outside of the microchurch meeting and help shepherd our microchurch flock.

Have them set up fellowship events outside of microchurch and teach them the importance of creating a sense of extended family with the microchurch.

Share meals with them in my home with my family and teach them about being a husband and a father as they see me interact with my family.

Share meals at restaurants and talk about witnessing to a waiter or waitress.

> The list goes on and on. The point is *let them into your life.* Do the things you love to do and bring them along with you. Give them leadership opportunities all the time. Let them succeed and then talk about it. Let them fail and then talk about it. Make sure you are taking every opportunity to teach them, no matter what you are doing. Be intentional with these discipleship moments!

Reflection Questions:
Leaving a Legacy

List out five creative ideas of how you are going to find the hungry, faithful, and fruitful members of your microchurch (at least one in each category)

What are your strengths as a leader? What do you enjoy doing as a leader?

What are your weaknesses? What do you not like doing as a leader?

How can you delegate out your weaknesses in a way that benefits the microchurch?

What is hard for you to delegate as a leader? Why is it important to be diligent as a delegating microchurch leader even in the areas you are strong in?

What are some ways you could invite an apprentice into your life outside of just seeing them at microchurch?

Multiplication: SETTING UP FOR SUCCESS

Step 1:

Commit Yourself to Multiplication (Make Your Mother Cry)

I still remember moving into my college dorm. It was the first time that I had moved away from home and into a season of life where I flexed my independence and was on my own. My mom and step-dad helped move me into my dorm at the University of Florida; room 315 in Graham Hall. I did not have a lot of stuff so the move was pretty short and easy. I said my goodbyes to my mom and step-dad and started unpacking. Little did I know (until years later) that my mom stood in the parking lot for about fifteen minutes looking up at my little dorm room on the third floor crying like baby. In fact, the only reason she actually left was because my step-dad said, "Okay Lynne, time to go. If he were to look down here and see you..." It would have been a young college freshman's nightmare. I never would have lived that down!

Even though my mom was sad and I was nervous moving out and starting college, we both knew it was the right thing to do. We had talked about it and although it was going to be tough for my mom to lose another child to college and a challenge for me to learn how to live independently, we both recognized this was the best thing for me.

You see most of us don't like change. Some of us stay in the same rut forever because we are too scared to obey what God is calling us to step out and do. But when we let God call the shots and we live for His Kingdom and not ours, even the toughest decisions He asks us to make are the best ones for us.

Multiplication can be one of those tough, get-you-out-of-your-comfort-zone decisions. It is like going to college: at first, it is really tough for you and your parents. But after you start to see the benefits of it, you wonder why you ever doubted it in the first place. Sure it would be easier for the apprentice to stay with his/her microchurch leader and continue to be the dynamic duo, but it isn't the best thing for the apprentice, the microchurch leader, or the microchurch. Apprentices are raised up so they can become leaders, not so they can wait in the wings for the rest of their lives. (Jesus called us to GO and make disciples, not stay where you are.) A microchurch leader needs to start pouring into others and raising them up. And if the microchurch is growing and vibrant, more people are going to want to come, and eventually the microchurch is going to run out of space. People will eventually be turned away due to a lack of space, or people will get lost in the crowd of 30+ people each week. So instead of waiting for people to start dropping out of the microchurch and discipleship to get stagnant and inwardly focused, we multiply. We start fresh. We allow room for new people to come in and experience the community that has so changed our lives.

THE FIRST STEP TO EFFECTIVELY MULTIPLYING IS TO ACKNOWLEDGE THE KINGDOM BENEFIT OF MULTIPLICATION. MULTIPLICATION IS THE BEST THING FOR THE APPRENTICE, THE MICROCHURCH LEADER, AND THE MICROCHURCH TO STAY VIBRANT, HEALTHY, AND GROWING.

Step 2: **Dethrone Yourself**

Leadership is hard. Especially if you are good at it. I don't know about you, but I am a perfectionist. If I have a vision for how I want something to go, I want it executed that way. I used to say to myself, "I'll just do it. That way I know it will get done right." Can you relate to that at all? Most high caliber leaders have strong vision and are gifted enough to make that happen. But do you remember the D word from a few chapters back? Delegation. This is what separates good microchurch leaders from great microchurch leaders: the ability to delegate and get others involved in the leadership of your microchurch.

One of the biggest indicators of whether or not a leader is primed for multiplication is something that usually goes unnoticed by the untrained eye. It is an all-encompassing element of the microchurch that somehow does not get brought up very often. Most people will come to your microchurch and fall into line without even realizing it, accepting this as the status quo, not to be trifled with. When all is said and done, you as the leader are completely responsible for it, because it is your call to make. So what is this component of your microchurch that carries so much weight when it comes to multiplication?

IT IS THE WAY YOU STRUCTURE YOUR MICROCHURCH.

The way your microchurch is set up says a lot about your leadership style. Are you the one calling all the shots? Do you do all the talking? Does anyone else have a chance to teach or speak? Do you come up with all the ideas? How involved are others, such as apprentices? How much say do they have in, well, anything?

These are good questions to ask yourself as a leader. How much of this is on me to pull off? Is there even a way for anyone else to jump into the leadership of my microchurch? Is the microchurch based exclusively upon me?

There is not a one-size-fits-all type approach to multiplication, or even a one-perfect-way to structure a microchurch for multiplication. There are, however, key things that you can do to dethrone yourself from the epicenter of leadership in your microchurch and help prepare it for multiplication success.

Let me give you some structural examples:

A traditional Bible Study looks like this:

- 5 minutes of fellowship and snacks that the leader provides
- 20 minutes of worship by leader or a member of the Bible study
- 40 minutes of the leader sharing a teaching from the Word
- 5 minutes for prayer requests written down/ emailed out by the leader.

This type of structure week in and week out is not conducive to multiplication. Why? It is because you, the leader, are still on the leadership throne in all areas of the evening. So how could we open this up a bit to make it more conducive to multiplication? Let's look at this again:

A Bible Study style microchurch with multiplication in mind looks like this:

- 5 minutes of fellowship and snacks

- **Snacks delegated to one of the microchurch members**

- 20 minutes of worship

- **Have multiple people rotate leading worship**

- 40 minutes of the leader sharing a teaching from the Word

- **Each week have a different person lead the discussion OR have multiple breakout discussions going on led by different people at the same time**

- 15 minutes for prayer requests

- **Have people break out into the same prayer groups each week and have them be responsible for following up with one another OR have a point person each week volunteer to email out the prayer requests to everyone else**

Notice the difference here: multiple people own each aspect of the microchurch. If the leader did not show up, the microchurch would go on without him/her, which is a multiplication WIN! When kids grow up and start providing for themselves, parents don't usually get mad. In fact, that is usually when the parents do a celebratory dance of financial freedom! Same thing with a microchurch: as a leader, you WANT independence and ownership outside of your leadership. If you can't celebrate this, then you have control issues that need to be dealt with because they are not Christ-centered. Just remember, it is not your kingdom to begin with, so stop structuring your microchurch like it is!!

If you won't make that switch, then God will ensure that it happens... at least that was what happened to me! Earlier in my career as a microchurch leader, I was at a place in my life where I was working, trying to finish up my Master's degree, dealing with intense family drama, and other life situations that inevitably come at the worst time. Prepping for microchurch had slipped down the ladder of importance and I found myself completely overwhelmed by the responsibility of creating and leading a teaching every week, doing worship, following up with all the members of my microchurch, getting my house ready each week, and all the other tasks that come along with leading a microchurch. I couldn't keep up. I was burning out.

So out of desperation (and poor leadership), I approached my microchurch and told them I was at the end of my rope and if something didn't change we were going to stop meeting. We brainstormed ways the microchurch could become an easier yoke for me and be just as effective or even better.

What came out of this conversation was the idea of what we dubbed "tiny groups." The purpose was two-fold: 1. To have gender-based accountability groups that do not change week to week. (This way, you can have people consistently agreeing with you in prayer and holding you accountable each week.) 2. To rotate the leadership of the microchurch each month from tiny group to tiny group. This way, everyone has a chance to lead, participate, and use their gifts. Plus, when responsibility rests with a tiny group of 4-6 other people, the burden is not too heavy on any one person.

Tiny groups also facilitate different passions and callings that might otherwise be overlooked. I have found that some people love to worship, so every time their tiny group is leading we have a God-night, focused on worship. Others are very evangelistic, so whenever their tiny group leads we know we are going to go out and do some evangelism! But the neat thing is everyone has a voice, everyone has an opportunity to lead, and everyone is involved in the culture and life of the microchurch.

It has been the best model I have seen in regard to keeping the microchurch lively and exciting without losing the fundamentals of why we meet: to know God through His Word and through prayer and discipleship while growing in community both inside and out. Here is a diagram of how leadership looks like in my microchurch. (Remember green nights from chapter 2? If not, take a quick peek as a reference.)

For more information on tiny groups and how to implement this microchurch structure and strategy, check out Appendix A

Month 1: Tiny Group #1 Leads

W1, Core Night (Colossians 1)

W2, Green Night: Either worship, community, or mission focused

W3, Core Night (Colossians 2)

W4, Green Night: Either worship, community, or mission focused

Month 2: Tiny Group #2 Leads

W1, Core Night (Colossians 3)

W2, Green Night: Either worship, community, or mission focused

W3, Core Night (Colossians 4)

W4, Green Night: Either worship, community, or mission focused

Month 3: Tiny Group #3 Leads

W1, Core Night (Ruth 1)

W2, Green Night: Either worship, community, or mission focused

W3, Core Night (Ruth 2)

W4, Green Night: Either worship, community, or mission focused

Month 4: Tiny Group #4 Leads

W1, Core Night (Ruth 3)

W2, Green Night: Either worship, community, or mission focused

W3, Core Night (Ruth 4)

W4, Green Night: Either worship, community, or mission focused

STRUCTURE YOUR MICROCHURCH IN A WAY THAT IS
CONDUCIVE TO DELEGATION AND MULTIPLICATION.
AS A LEADER, YOUR JOB IS TO BE EXPENDABLE AND
HAVE AN ARMY OF APPRENTICES RAISED UP TO TAKE
YOUR PLACE AT ANY GIVEN MOMENT!

Step 3:

Receive the Triad of Confirmation

Is anyone reading this not a fan of school? Did you
ever dream or scheme about how to graduate
from high school or college early? You know it
is probably a good thing that we, the students,
don't get to dictate when we graduate. If this
were the case, a lot of us would have graduated
way too early. And those who are big nerds and
love academics (myself included) might have
stayed in school for the rest of our lives!

When it comes to multiplication it is important to
figure out the right time to multiply, and the most
important element that determines the right time
for multiplication is if your apprentice is ready to
lead a microchurch. I repeat, the most important
piece leading up to multiplication is if your
apprentice is ready. I don't care how many people
you have coming to your microchurch. I don't care
how much the Holy Spirit is flowing. I don't care how
excited people are. These are all good things, but
your multiplication will fall flat if you send out an
apprentice who is not yet ready to lead.

THERE IS REAL DANGER IN NOT BEING WISE ABOUT
THE TIMING OF RELEASING AN APPRENTICE.

Too early: My microchurch has currently multiplied seven times.   Five of those microchurches are still healthy and strong to this day. We have four microchurch babies and even have one microchurch grandbaby (a multiplication from one of our multiplications). If you were counting, you'd realize that means two didn't make it. These were our first two attempts at multiplication. The first was a leader who was biting at the bit to lead. He was anxious to start leading and so we decided to rush into releasing him since he was so excited and hungry. He eventually was overwhelmed with the responsibility of leadership and bowed out a few months later due to a lack of understanding of what to expect, since we did not take the time to properly equip him. The other leader I sent out too early without testing his faithfulness and although he was a great leader, it wasn't the right season for him to be leading. That microchurch only lasted a few months before he threw in the towel.

IN MANY CASES, THE APPRENTICE MAY NEVER FEEL 100% PREPARED, AND THIS IS TO BE EXPECTED. BUT IT CAN ALSO BE JUST AS DANGEROUS TO PROLONG THE APPRENTICESHIP.

Too late: On the flip side of things, you may have an apprentice who doesn't want to leave the nest. These apprentices are usually meticulous, careful and err on the side of caution. He/she doesn't want to go until every single duck is in a row. Perfectly. They will never be 100% prepared, but ask any new parent whether they felt 100% prepared to have that first baby! There is always an amount of risk and fear, but hopefully along with that comes faith and a reliance on God.

The true sign of an apprentice being ready and the healthy precursor to an effective multiplication is the triad of confirmation. This three-part confirmation comes when:

1. You, the leader, feel that the apprentice is ready.

2. The apprentice also feels that he/she is ready.

3. Through prayer, wisdom, and discernment you receive confirmation through the Holy Spirit.

In Acts 15:28, the leaders of the early church were attempting to figure out the fusion of Gentiles into the Christian faith. What requirements did they need to keep from the Jewish heritage of Christianity? There were a lot of thoughts on this and a lot of heresies that came from trying to figure this out. The early church leaders needed wisdom and I love the way they phrased their eventual response: "It seemed good to the Holy Spirit and to us..."

This is the three-part confirmation we are looking for: it seemed good to the Holy Spirit and to us (in this case, the microchurch leader and apprentice). When everyone is united and on the same page, the time is probably right, and you are on your way to a healthy, vibrant multiplication!

Reflection Questions: Primed and Ready!

List out at least three key points you would share with members of your microchurch about why multiplication is a good thing

What are some ways you are going to structure your microchurch so that it is primed and ready for multiplication?

List five different signs that would lead you to believe that your apprentice is ready to multiply and lead his/her own microchurch.

THROWING PARTIES, PRAYING PRAYERS

The best part about a graduation is the party, which usually includes a lot of great food and a lot of fun celebrating the accomplishment with some of your closest friends! This is also one of my absolute favorite parts about multiplication: the wild parties we throw to celebrate the accomplishment! Now my wife and I take these parties very seriously. You are not allowed in the door unless you are dressed according to the theme. We have had an 80's party, 70's party, a pirate party, and more! We go all out and have a blast. We have even had party crashers! We have parties because we are celebrating new life, a new microchurch, and an apprentice who is stepping into what God has for them in this new season of ministry and leadership.

We play hard, but we also pray hard. When we look at Biblical models of people being raised up for leadership, we see an all-pervasive theme running through each example: prayer. Paul models this again and again for us with his apprentices. He seemed to always lay his hands on the apprentice and pray over his life and leadership.

> ### 1st Timothy 4:14
>
> "Do not neglect your gift, which was given you through prophecy when the body of elders laid their hands on you."

> ### 2nd Timothy 1:6
>
> "For this reason I remind you to fan into flame the gift of God, which is in you through the laying on of my hands."

When someone steps into leadership, they are increasing their influence and impact and are committing to give themselves to leading others in Gospel-centered lives. This is a huge deal and something we don't want our leaders to forget, or think that they are stepping into alone. It is important to bathe the multiplication in prayer, but also to commission the new apprentice with the laying on of hands and with the blessing of the microchurch leader. So make sure the celebration includes a time for the microchurch leader and all the microchurch members pray for, encourage, and bless the new up and coming leader!

THERE'S NO "RIGHT " WAY TO MULTIPLY

There is no set way to multiply. Multiplication is usually tailored to the microchurch's unique situation. Very rarely will multiplications look the same. Be creative! Find ways that would best fit your microchurch's situation. Address the specific needs and desires of your microchurch and lead them in one of the following ways:

LEADER　　 **APPRENTICE**　　 **MEMBER**

TRADITIONAL MULTIPLICATION

Your microchurch multiplies into two groups, one which is led by you, the original microchurch leader, and the other led by your apprentice. The new microchurch simply takes half of the original microchurch members and begins a new microchurch at a different location.

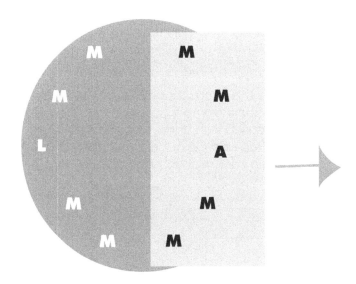

MICROCHURCH PLANT

If you have an apprentice that is ready to lead his or her own microchurch, but you don't have enough people to multiply in the traditional sense, then you may want to think about sending the apprentice out to plant a microchurch. The microchurch planter may maintain a relationship with the original microchurch and may even continue to attend the original microchurch, if it meets on a different night.

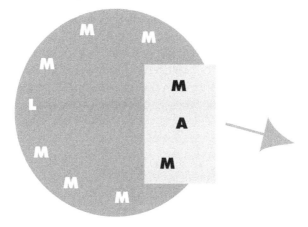

APOSTOLIC MULTIPLICATION

If you as the microchurch leader enjoy forming and creating new groups, you can also leave your microchurch under the leadership of your apprentice and go out on your own and begin forming a new microchurch altogether.

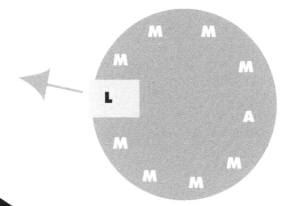

MICROCHURCH LAUNCH

This method of multiplication involves creating and launching a leadership core from your microchurch and having them start a microchurch of their own. The launch group will be significantly smaller than the group that remains with the original leader. For example, a microchurch of 20 might launch a leadership team of 5 to form a new microchurch while the 15 remain with the original group. This is very similar to Internal Multiplication, but in this case, there is not one person who has invited the other four or five people. The people starting the new microchurch are chosen by the leader to launch out.

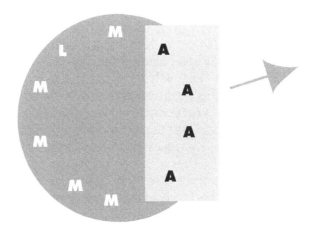

AGAIN, ANY WAY TO MULTIPLY IS GOOD. GET CREATIVE AND DO WHAT WORKS BEST FOR YOUR MICROCHURCH!

For me personally, tiny groups have been the best discovery I have ever made in regard to multiplication of microchurches. The hard work is already done for you. From day one, I set up my microchurch to have gender-based accountability groups. Even if there are only six people, we are going to break into two gender based tiny groups and start using the tiny group method of leading microchurch. I create that culture early so people know what to expect as we grow and add more members. As soon as we have sixteen people in our microchurch, we break out into four tiny groups and continue with the strategy mentioned in the tiny group section.

The goal is to have four tiny groups so that when we get big enough to multiply, we simply send two of the tiny groups out to start meeting in another place. (This is the same set up as a traditional multiplication, just with the added element of tiny groups). Having these strong connections in the tiny groups helps everyone feel like they are not leaving all their friends because the people you are most connected to, those in your tiny groups, are going with you! Plus, there is not as much fear for your apprentice to take over the new microchurch since he or she is used to and has been practicing the tiny group leadership model for months now. There is really no change in the way the microchurch is run... the only difference is a new location!

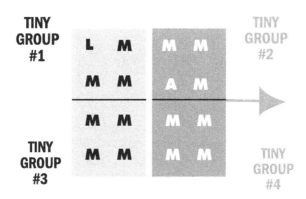

Reflection Questions: Launching Out!

How do you know which multiplication style is right for you?

How can you ensure that your apprentice feels covered before the launch?

What are some ways to make sure they are covered after the launch?

What are some things that you can do as the leader to give your apprentice the best chance to succeed with his/her new microchurch?

AFTER WORD

Legacy.

What a powerful word. It is what is left of you when you are gone. It represents your life effort and the effectiveness of how well you pulled it off. I believe one of the most important questions that is going to be asked on judgment day as we stand before Jesus is, "How many disciples did you make?" So let me ask you a personal question; how many disciples have you made up to this point in your life? I am not talking about how many spiritual conversations you had or how many times you sort of helped someone out. That wasn't the question.

HOW MANY DISCIPLES HAVE YOU MADE?

How many people can point to you as one of the primary catalysts for their spiritual growth because of the time, prayer, teaching, and life-on-life moments that you shared together? It is a sobering question but one of the most important questions you will ever ask yourself. This isn't a condemnation trip; this is a call to spend yourself for things that have eternal weight and value!

To say no to worldly pursuits that are not going to matter even one year from now, much less one million years from now. The question isn't going to be how many movies you watched, how many sports stats you can rattle off, how many likes you got on Facebook, or how many sweet recipes you pulled off Pinterest. The question that matters is this; how many disciples have you made?

What will you be remembered for? My earnest prayer is that you as a microchurch leader will be remembered for the discipleship legacy you left in your wake. Don't waste your life, friend. Don't waste your life!!! This is the rallying cry: spend yourself for the things that matter most. This is the call to let the beauty of the Gospel inconvenience your comfortable life with the messiness that comes when you're discipling others. Give yourself to the Gospel! Give yourself to disciple making!

GIVE YOURSELVES TO THE ONE WHO GAVE HIMSELF FOR YOU. IT ONLY SEEMS FITTING, IN LIGHT OF HIS MERCY, TO OFFER YOURSELF RIGHT BACK TO HIM...

I want to share with you a chart that I look at often. I am an introvert and I have aspirations that run so deep to do great things for the One who has done such great things for and in me. I weep regularly at the thought of wanting so badly to make my life count, not because I want to leave a legacy per say, but because I want to show my appreciation for what Jesus has done for me. I want others to taste and see He is good. Sometimes, however, I would get overwhelmed because I thought, "What can I do?"

NUMBER OF MICROCHURCHES	NUMBER OF 👤 PER MICROCHURCH	TOTAL NUMBER OF 👤👤👤
1	20	20
2	20	40
4	20	80
8	20	160
16	20	320
32	20	640
64	20	1,280
128	20	2,560
256	20	5,120
512	20	10,240
1,024	20	20,480
2,048	20	40,960
4,096	20	81,920
8,192	20	163,840

But then I started thinking, "If I give myself, truly give myself, to multiplying my microchurch once a year and raising up disciples who have that same passion to raise up other disciples who will go and multiply microchurches, then *I can make a radical difference. I can leave a substantial discipleship legacy.*"

Think about it. Take a look at that chart one more time. If you continue to multiply your microchurch (let's say the average is twenty people in each microchurch) every year and the ones who multiply from your microchurch do the same, within a span of a decade you will have reached over 10,000 people. Within fourteen years, over 160,000. Now I know this sounds like a pyramid scheme, but don't miss the point: as a microchurch leader, you have the unbridled potential to change the world by making disciples who make disciples and multiplying microchurches that multiply microchurches. When you go to rallies and hear, "Let's take this city for Jesus!!" that battle cry ceases to be mere hyperbole and becomes a tangible possibility when you think of it this way. It can be done. It will be done. And you can be the one to spark the flame that sets the entire city on fire.

Microchurch leaders, are you waiting for a sign? Then consider this your sign. Consider this your call. Consider this the starting point for the most important decision you will ever make; the decision to give yourself to changing the world one disciple at a time. Set your gaze and give yourself completely... not to results, but to the One who completely gave Himself for you. Get ready for the ride of your life that you will never forget and you will never regret.

Live a life worth following. Live a life worth remembering. Live in complete surrender to Him and watch Him do things you never thought possible in and through you.

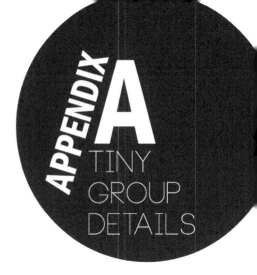

HOW TO CHOOSE TINY GROUPS

In order for tiny groups to be effective, you will want to put the people who have the most potential into the tiny groups that you are not leading. That way they have an opportunity to take leadership in that tiny group. Here are a few other pointers when forming tiny groups:

- Form the tiny groups around the people you think have the most potential to be future leaders. Then pair up people that have relational connections with each other. Ex. If Jack brought Frank and they are best friends, put them in the same tiny group

- I also give out a tiny group questionnaire to each member (see next page for an example). I form the tiny groups based on members' response to these questionnaires so that each person has a voice in their tiny group placement.

- It is easiest if you write out each person's name on a 3x5 card, or post it note, and spread the names out on the table. Then move the names to match people who have relational connections based on the questionnaire. Move them around and play with them until you figure out the best fit.

● Break them up by gender. I would try to keep
4 tiny groups (ideally 2 male and 2 female) at
the most. If you have more girls than guys for
example, then you can make more than 2 female
tiny groups. Try not to have more than 7 or so in a
tiny group to begin with so there is room to grow
when new people come!

LEADING IN THE TINY GROUP STRUCTURE

● Let the tiny groups lead, but the first few months
you are going to have to coach them through the
process of leading. For example, you will need to
remind them to send out emails to let everyone
know what you will be doing this coming week,
making sure they have a plan for the upcoming
week, etc. Trust me though; it is worth the extra
effort in the beginning because the long term
results are so good!

● On the core nights (when your tiny group is
not leading), always make sure you have a few
questions ready for discussion just in case the tiny
group hits a rough patch and no one is responding.
Let them lead, but be ready to help out when they
need it.

TINY **GROUP**
QUESTIONNAIRE

NAME

EMAIL

PHONE NUMBER

Circle the question below that is the MOST
IMPORTANT thing to you in regards to being in a
tiny group with other people from microchurch.

1 When are you available besides Tuesday
night to meet with others from microchurch?
  •

2 Who are the 2 people who you feel most
comfortable opening up with or have
relationships with already?

1.

2.

CIRCLE ONE

3 Single   Engaged   Married

4 Undergrad   Grad School   Working

5 Where do you live? (address and NW, SW,
NE, SE)

Made in United States
Orlando, FL
14 March 2023

31042219R00050